One More Thing...

ELDA ROBINSON,
INTERNATIONAL BEST-SELLING AUTHOR

PHOTOS BY **ANDY ROBINSON**

ONE MORE THING...

Copyright © 2024 by Elda Robinson

Sea Mist Imaginations

All photographs in this book were taken by Andrew Robinson. The illustration for "Homework" is from a picture done by a former student, Morgan Rotenberry.

All rights reserved. No part of this publication may be reproduced distributed or transmitted in any form or by any means including photocopying recording or other electronic or mechanical means without proper written permission of author or publisher, except in the case of brief quotations embodied in critical reviews and certain other noncommercial uses permitted by copyright law.

ISBN 978-1-7375752-2-1 (paperback)
ISBN 978-1-7375752-3-8 (hardcover)

Printed in the United States of America.

WHAT PEOPLE ARE SAYING

"When a teacher loves their students as if they are their own children, they see them more deeply, speak to them more wisely, and cherish them without end."
—Shelby Kottemann, internationally bestselling author, Reiki master, and founder of Love's Nature LLC

"The lessons and the messages are life-affirming and apply to everyone!"
—Misti Mazurik, lifelong learner, director of operations at RHG Media

"It brings hope to your heart and joy to your soul.... This is a book I could read again and again and learn new things about myself each time."
—Tiffani Freckleton, RN; award-winning bestselling author of *My NICU Story: Written With Love*; contributor, *Letters to a Future Nurse*

"Dive into One More Thing for a treasure trove of wisdom on embracing positivity, learning from the past, and living with gratitude."
—Maureen Ryan Blake, founder, Maureen Ryan Blake Media

DEDICATION

To all our students who have decorated our lives with more joy and awe at your abilities than any frustration or sorrow we felt at your "misses." We need to tell you just *One More Thing*.

CONTENTS

What people are saying 3

Dedication 5

Be good to yourselves 8

Never give up 10

Be willing to fail (sometimes spectacularly) 12

But know when to quit! 14

Read the road signs! *Detour* 16

Read the road signs! *Crossroads* 18

Read the road signs! *Stop* 20

Read the road signs! *Yield* 22

Read the road signs! *Curves ahead* 24

Listen 26

Quiet—be still 28

Break the rules! 30

Do the unexpected! 32

Focus 34

Live abundantly 36

Laugh 38

Choose your heroes carefully 40

Explore 42

CONTENTS

Sometimes teachers repeat things! 44

Homework 46

Bulletin board quotes 48

About the authors 50

Andrew Robinson 50

Elda Robinson 51

Reviews 53

BE GOOD TO YOURSELVES

BE GOOD TO YOURSELVES

After suffering a miscarriage, we realized that we needed to be the best we could be so that, if God did bless us with children, we would be the best possible parents. Less than a year later, we moved to California and began our Christian Education careers. You came into our classrooms in a variety of shapes, sizes, and personalities. You were scared, nervous, confident, ready to learn, yearning for recess or lunch, and "checked out." We told you that you were good and needed to be good to yourself.

When you were in our classrooms, you belonged to us. We weren't perfect, but we prayed for you and guided you to the best of our ability at the time. We look at our first years of teaching and think, "Oh, those poor kids having to deal with us!" And God did bless us with many "kids" during our almost fifty years in Christian education. You still are our kids. We remember our first classes at Community Christian in Red Bluff. We ran off worksheets on used computer paper and told you to step over the baby snake as you went to recess and then realized it was a rattlesnake! We stacked the desks on Fridays and set them up on Mondays. We remember the many prayers when we had our son and the big sign with a hot air balloon and all the signatures when we left.

Please be good to yourself! Stop comparing, stop dwelling on failures, stop living in the past, and, in the words of Judy Garland, "Always be a first-rate version of yourself and not a second-rate version of someone else."

NEVER GIVE UP

One of the joys of teaching was seeing that "aha" moment when you "got it" when you tried. That moment and feeling will never happen if you quit.

Mr. R played the part of Thomas Edison in one of the plays we did in Paradise. His song was "Never Give Up." Thomas Edison tried almost a thousand times before his idea for a light bulb worked! Call it perseverance, persistence, or stubbornness. You need to have a big dose of that in your life.

Mrs. R won't ever forget a young man she taught while at Monte Vista. That brave young man had serious vision issues, but he braved the hike and the dark cave at Pinnacles National Park and succeeded. There were many like him in our classrooms who didn't give up. Don't give up! And, if you have, start again!

When Mrs. R was teaching kindergarten, a student came to her desk and told her he couldn't do the alphabet letters for the day. She pulled out the page he did the first day of school. The student denied it was his until he saw his name written at the top. He smiled, confidently walked back to his desk, and finished his work. Are you tempted to quit? Take the time to see how far you have come. Mr. R has been known to say, "Anything worth doing is worth doing badly the first few times." Remember, "I can't do that" needs to be "I can't do that *yet*."

BE WILLING TO FAIL
(SOMETIMES SPECTACULARLY)

BE WILLING TO FAIL (SOMETIMES SPECTACULARLY)

One of the biggest joys of our retirement is being able to watch the ocean waves at Boiler Bay. One day we stopped there and got into a discussion about the waves. We became aware of the rhythm of the waves: a set of big waves, then some calming, and then back to big waves. We also noticed the waves never really succeeded!

The world measures success by how high you have climbed on the ladder, how much money you make, or how many "toys" you have. But God doesn't judge us that way. In 1 Corinthians, Paul reminds us to be faithful. Be faithful! Be faithful to yourself and to the abilities God gave you.

One of the first jobs Mr. Robinson had when he graduated from college was teaching PE to mentally challenged children and adults. One of their tasks was to step on the knot at the end of a hanging rope and try to climb. One adult tried every day and failed for at least six months before he finally was able to get both feet off the ground.

This is a life lesson, not just an academic school lesson. Be willing to lose, to fail in whatever you try at whatever age. Abraham Lincoln failed many times before he became one of our most beloved presidents. Isaac Newton failed miserably at farming. Steven Spielberg was rejected by USC Cinematic Arts School, not once but twice. Walt Disney was told he had no imagination! Elvis Presley was told to go back to truck driving when he first appeared at the Grand Ole Opry.

BUT KNOW WHEN TO QUIT!

We know what you're thinking: "Hey! Didn't you just tell us to not quit?" So why are we now saying you should know when to quit? Simple. Sometimes the best move is to quit. There is a Chinese proverb that says, "Of all the stratagems, to know when to quit is the best."

Sometime *quit* means quit, and sometimes it means stop and take a break. Know when to stop. Both Mr. R and Mrs. R told students to study about twenty minutes and then take a break. Why? Because that is about all that your mind and body can take. Sometimes it is even a shorter amount of time. We both cringed when we heard students say, "I studied hours for the test." Truthfully, you wasted a lot of time. But sometimes there is a time limit, so don't wait until the last minute. There are always computer issues when you wait. Know the difference between stopping for awhile and quitting completely.

Dr. Adina Silvestri has compiled a list of things to immediately quit. Here they are:

1. Quit trying to please everyone.
2. Quit putting yourself down.
3. Quit living in the past.
4. Quit fearing change.
5. Quit overthinking.

That is excellent advice. Maybe you could add some others to this list, but start with those. Know when and what to quit.

READ THE ROAD SIGNS!

DETOUR

Sometimes we had to take detours. We called them "rabbit trails," but most of the time they were stories to help you understand the concept. And we know that you students loved to get us to go down rabbit trails!

Detours in life can come unexpectedly. We are moving along, things are going nicely, and then *WHAM*—a detour! It can be just about anything that disrupts our daily routine.

Sometimes the detour comes because we need to work on patience or we need to slow down. Sometimes the detour takes us around a hazard. A blogger said, "Sometimes God slows you down so the evil ahead of you will pass before you get there. Your delay could mean your protection [...]." Sometimes there seems to be no reason for them, but there they are!

Normally, we gripe and grumble when we come across a detour. The usual response is "Oh no, what now?" What would happen if we embrace the detour? Who knows? There might be something interesting to see and learn. After all, you are going to have to take that detour, like it or not. You might as well get the most out of it.

And don't forget to smile at the road workers. Think about all the negativity they experience just trying to do their jobs.

READ THE ROAD SIGNS!

CROSSROADS

Mr. R's goal growing up was to go into radio or TV broadcasting. His dad told him he needed to go to Bible College for a year before he did that. He was accepted at Western Baptist Bible College in El Cerrito, California. After his first year, he came home and worked all summer to get money for college. His dad asked him where he was going, and he said, "Western!" He went back that next year and met Mrs. R.

Mrs. R has always loved science and music. Her goal was to go into medical technology and eventually cancer research. She was going to go to Western for one year and then transfer to another college for her medical studies. That one year at Western was when she met Mr. R.

Our goals changed! We wouldn't want to go back to those old goals. So don't be afraid to let go of old goals and turn in a different direction if that is where God is leading.

Crossroads can be a slight jog. Those are easier and less scary! During pledges at school, you quoted Psalm 119:105 almost every day. "Your Word is a lamp to my feet and a light to my path." Lights can show the way just in front of us—the next steps. Lamps are held high to shine out in the darkness and show the future path. Lights are for the slight jogs to avoid nearby pitfalls, whereas lamps show the direction we should be going. Both are valuable tools in living our lives meaningfully and to the fullest. We may not end up where we thought we were going, but if we pay attention to the road signs, we end up where we are supposed to be.

READ THE ROAD SIGNS!

STOP

I found this powerfully enabling quote from Bob Marley: "God sent me on earth. He send me to do something, and nobody can stop me. If God want to stop me, then I stop. Man never can." And for my North Hills high school English students, yes, he said "He send me"!

Remember playing "Red Light, Green Light" at recess? Sometimes we need to heed the warning of others without questioning or ignoring what they are saying. Mr. R often shared a story of a missionary family who lived in an area that had very venomous snakes. One day as their child was playing outside, the mother noticed a snake hanging from a tree. The mother calmly told the child to stop and come to her. He obeyed immediately, and the snake dropped to the ground where the child had been.

There were times on the Paradise coast trip when you needed to do what you were told immediately. Remember dashing over the rocks to avoid getting wet? Or how about the infamous "elk walk"? (This was where we had our students walk carefully and silently past the Roosevelt elk that was on our path to keep them safe from any danger.)

Many ignore the signs and warnings, speed through dangerous curves, and ignore the fences that are set up to protect. Sadly, some of them pay a very high price for such ignorance. If you get a gut feeling something isn't right, see the signs, or hear "Don't do it!", it is best to obey immediately.

READ THE ROAD SIGNS!

YIELD

Yielding is challenging. Yielding requires us to focus on the present and observe what is transpiring. It means maybe not being in control!

In a beginner adult swim class, Mr. R had a student who was extremely afraid to put his face in the water. One week, Mr. R brought a large mixing bowl to class and filled it with pool water. The man watched and was then encouraged to bend over and put the tip of his nose in the bowl of water. He was reluctant at first but was able to bend forward and touch his nose to the water. He was then encouraged to pinch his nose shut and try it again, this time getting more of his nose wet. Finally, after much encouragement from others in the class, he said, "I am going to go for it." Pinching his nose again, he put his face completely into the bowl. When he sat up, he smiled and said that it wasn't so bad. Sometimes all you have to do is put your fears aside and "go for it."

When Mrs. R's mother was eighty years old, she told her daughter, "I am not asking your permission, I am telling you I am moving to Hawaii." She had lived in Northern California her whole life, and on a small farm for sixty years! She felt God saying "Go," so she did! Those remaining three years of her life were filled with joy and usefulness.

Don't be afraid to change directions or try something different. If God says "Go," then GO—at full speed and with confidence!

READ THE ROAD SIGNS!

CURVES AHEAD

READ THE ROAD SIGNS!

Let's start with a quote from Iyanla Vanzant: "You know why the road curves as you're driving along? It curves because if God showed us the distance from where we are to where we're going, we'd think it was too far." Isn't that so like us? "Are we there yet?" . . . "How much farther is it?" . . . "I can't wait that long. Curves make me sick!" Those of you who ever rode with Mr. R know that a set of tight curves often became straightened when he drove!

You are still going the right direction when the road curves, just not in a straight line. And, trust us, life is never in a straight line. Mr. R can talk about heart attacks because he knows the subject personally. Mrs. R can talk about living with baldness because she lives it. There are things in life that happen to us that can make us stronger, wiser, and better able to help others (if we let them). It requires talking authentically, with integrity. Another way of saying this is that you must walk the talk! You must live truthfully, honestly. If you don't, then you could be called a hypocrite. And, contrary to popular opinion, hypocrites are found everywhere, not just in churches!

I found this great quote by Mae West: "Cultivate your curves—they may be dangerous but they won't be avoided." If you know who she was, you will see the humor as well as the truth of this statement.

LISTEN

"Listen or your tongue will make you deaf." That quote is credited to Terri Farley, though I read it in a book that attributes it to Native Americans. Whoever said it, they were very wise.

Amazing things can be heard if you stop anticipating what you are going to reply and quietly listen. That was true in every school we ministered. When we took the time to listen, sometimes to what was not said, we understood your pain and frustrations a little more.

Elijah stood before King Ahab and told him it wasn't going to rain until he (Elijah) said so. And it didn't. After a few years he told Ahab, "Let's have a contest to see which god is greater, yours or mine." Remember the outcome? Ahab's priests prayed all day trying to get their gods to answer them. Elijah then prayed a short prayer, and God answered with fire. Elijah told everyone, "Head home; it's going to rain." And, after some more prayer, it poured!

After that victory, Elijah ran from Jezebel because he got scared. He was tired and feeling sorry for himself. Remember how God talked to him? First he fed him, then he told him to rest, and then he answered in a quiet voice, not with thunder and lightning. He encouraged Elijah quietly with some simple truths.

Remember, as both Mr. R and Mrs. R said in their classrooms, "God gave you two ears and one mouth for a reason. Listen twice as much as you talk."

QUIET—BE STILL

I am sure both of us used these words a lot in our classrooms! It's actually part of listening. This world is so full of busyness that we often neglect the quiet. And yet, quiet is essential to growth. Think about the cycle of the seasons. Spring and summer are the times of renewed growth and fruitfulness. Fall and winter are the times for slowing down and gaining strength.

It is in the quiet that our souls are nourished, our vision clarified, our confidence strengthened and our resolve renewed. Isaiah 30:15 says, "in quietness and confidence I find my strength." We hear a lot about "burnout." It can be caused by never taking time to be quiet and evaluate what you are doing, how you are doing it, and if you should be doing it.

Don't confuse busyness with productivity. A hamster is very busy on that wheel but doesn't produce anything of value. Make sure your busyness is productive and life-affirming. And make your quietness quiet, invigorating, and productive. Mrs. R went online to www.brainyquotes.com to see if there were any great quotes about relaxation. There were eleven pages of them! And, from all she read, it was clear that there are a variety of ways to relax. When do you feel most relaxed? Decide what works best, and then do it on a regular basis.

BREAK THE RULES!

BREAK THE RULES!

We met in a college located in El Cerrito, California. On weekends we would travel to minister at the Clayton Valley Church. Most of the time we squeezed into a classmate's car to get there.

One weekend, however, we went by ourselves on a borrowed motorcycle. Mrs. R's father had always been strongly against motorcycles, so riding a motorcycle felt like breaking the rules. We started out just fine, even though there was a lot of traffic. Then disaster hit! The motorcycle quit running. We were on the side of a busy freeway and didn't have a clue what to do. Our friends in the car ahead didn't see us, so we had to wait until a nice CHP officer came and helped us out. It was a bit stressful. And Mrs. R never told her parents about that weekend!

Choose wisely! Breaking some rules can be disastrous, but not always! Remember the story about Daniel's friends refusing to bow to the idol. They decided to follow the right way and were victoriously protected.

Here's a list of seven people who broke the rules for the right reason. I challenge you to look them up and read about what they did: Lilian Bland, Claudette Colvin, Johannes Gutenberg, Jovita Idar, Hedy Lamarr (beyond being a Hollywood star), Lewis Latimer, Witold Pilecki, and "Tank Man" (Tiananmen Square, 1989).

Our Watsonville cat, Chocolate, certainly broke the rules by taking a nap in the bird feeder!

DO THE UNEXPECTED!

DO THE UNEXPECTED!

We need to do some unexpected things in our lives. Although it might be a little difficult, the rewards include delight in yourself and contentment in your accomplishment. It can be exhilarating. Or you may not like it at all!

Don't be afraid to try something unexpected or new, but be smart about it. Afraid of heights? Maybe you shouldn't try skydiving. Allergic to some foods? Don't try eating them to see if anything has changed! But, usually, just because you have never _____ (fill in the blank) doesn't mean you shouldn't try it at least once. Yes, middle school choir girls at Monte Vista, Mrs. R still remembers you talking her into a roller coaster ride! She hasn't ridden one since!

One day a young man in Mrs. R's high school English class said he didn't want to be disrespectful, but he thought she and Mr. R were the kind to just go home and sit watching TV! He couldn't quite imagine someone our ages riding a motorcycle, flying in balloons, or digging dinosaur bones!

Now, in 2023, we don't do some of those things anymore, but we want you to know we still do the unexpected! We took a wild ride on a sand rail to celebrate our anniversary this year. Going 55 miles an hour up a steep sand dune was awesome! But keep your mouth closed.

Explore the possibilities found in doing the unexpected. We came to school on the motorcycle when we ministered in North Hills to fulfill a promise we made to the elementary students. They didn't know who we were until we took our helmets off!

FOCUS

Have you ever daydreamed in class? Have you ever been unsure how you got somewhere because you didn't remember the drive? Your mind just drifts away to other stuff, and you don't pay attention to what you are currently involved in. Mrs. R has to admit she did that during a literature class in high school and got her picture in the yearbook! Thankfully, no one knew what she was daydreaming about! If you want to live life fully and intentionally, you need to stay focused. Here is an awesome quote we wish we had known when we were teaching:

"We are always falling in love or quarreling, looking for jobs or fearing to lose them, getting ill and recovering, following public affairs. If we let ourselves, we shall always be waiting for some distraction or other to end before we can really get down to our work. The only people who achieve much are those who want knowledge so badly that they seek it while the conditions are still unfavorable. Favorable conditions never come." —C.S. Lewis, *The Weight of Glory*

It is interesting that "really get down to our work" is part of that quote. Being focused is for every facet of your life. If you lose focus, you may miss hazards, danger, or blessings. To really live life fully, you need to live "in the minute" with eternity's values in view. So—as teachers like to say—FOCUS!

LIVE ABUNDANTLY

There are seemingly endless quotes about abundance. However, I think one of the best is from Erma Bombeck. You want to know about her life? Look her up! She was a very popular humorist, but she also helped with advancing women's rights. This is her quote: "When I stand before God at the end of my life, I would hope that I would not have a single bit of talent left, and could say, 'I used everything you gave me.'" Don't waste any of the talents you have been given. In order to do that, you need to find out what your talents and abilities are.

Always be hungry to learn or experience something more. Never be afraid to ask "Why?", "What for?", "How?", "When?", or "What happens if...?". We both tried to encourage those questions in our classrooms. We weren't afraid to say, "I don't know, let's find out." In some schools, we had to do some library research. And in some schools we all logged in and looked up the answers online!

Don't stop learning. Textbooks tell you only the minimum amount. Learn more, and don't limit your learning to the first few hits on the search engine! And, because it is a hot-button issue with Mrs. R, learn how to read cursive so you can read primary sources.

Accomplishments, rewards, and recognition may come to those who maintain their curiosity and appetite for learning in a world where most mindlessly accept what is told them and never stop to wonder or question. The world of knowledge is constantly growing, so why not grow with it? Don't stunt your growth.

LAUGH

If you read our previous book, you know there is a section about laughing called "Jocularity." Life should include a big dose of silliness. Laughing at ourselves and laughing with others are two important ingredients in a life well lived. Notice we said laughing *with* others. As we told you when you were students, the difference between making fun and having fun is that one is enjoyed by only one person, whereas the other is enjoyed by both people. If both people aren't laughing, truly laughing, then something is wrong.

I saw a poster from LittleNivi.com that said, "Best thing about me? I laugh at my own jokes so you don't have to. But you probably will because I am hilarious." Laughing at ourselves is so freeing. Laugh often and loudly at yourself and with others.

The kids in Mrs. R's classes at Monte Vista knew they didn't have fun, they had "educational experiences." And Mr. R's classes were known to ~~endure~~ enjoy his jokes! (Oops!) King's Valley middle schoolers delighted in his dressing up in a tutu for Twin Day! Ygnacio Valley students smiled and enjoyed him taxiing a student around from class to class in his office chair as a reward. Then there were Rube Goldberg projects, Scooter Hockey, "popcorn" towers, silly songs, and science experiments.

CHOOSE YOUR HEROES CAREFULLY

CHOOSE YOUR HEROES CAREFULLY

Don't expect your heroes to always do right, but do expect your heroes to do right most of the time. Heroes come in all colors, shapes, sizes, and ages. They are often disguised as ordinary individuals. However, when their moment comes, they accomplish extraordinary things or they create a way for others to accomplish great things. The NYFD first responders did both on 9/11.

So, what makes a hero? There is a big difference between being a hero and being a celebrity. Celebrities are often considered heroes, but true heroes don't focus on themselves. An article by Philip Zimbardo reminds us that a hero's deed is done in the service of others, not self. He also says that heroes volunteer. Heroes step up while others step back. Heroes don't count the costs and possible consequences. Sometimes they act instinctively. They don't anticipate reward or recognition.

Our heroes can change as we grow. Mr. and Mrs. R have been blessed to have some lifelong heroes in their lives, from the nurse who reminded Mrs. R of God's love when she was having a miscarriage to the men who surrounded Mr. R and mentored him when he became a principal. They also have been inspired by the kindness, generosity, and tenacity of so many of their students.

So, who are your heroes? Who counts you as a hero?

EXPLORE

EXPLORE

When we moved from Wisconsin to California in 1979, we were challenged by Neil Smith, missionary to Brazil, to go and spend some time in Brazil as short-term missionaries. We had no money to get to Brazil, let alone spend some time there. We prayed about it and in less than two weeks we had all the money we needed for transportation and incidentals. We spent seven weeks that summer in Curitiba, Brazil, and we cherish every memory we have of that long-ago summer. "Deus e tao bom" (translation: "God is so good").

In order to live with the "Let's explore the possibilities" way of thinking, one must combine knowledge, wisdom and flexibility. One shouldn't go into any situation without some knowledge. We had no grasp of the Portuguese language, but we knew we would be helping at a seminary with construction and setting up a library.

The last leg of our flight was a Portuguese airline. We knew the flight attendant was asking what we wanted to drink, so we said Coke, a drink known worldwide. She handed us each a glass with a brownish drink with lots of foam. We sniffed it and sampled it, and it was really good. Turned out it was a soft drink called Guarana, and we enjoy it still today!

Those of you in Mr. R's classes in Paradise may remember a game called Hexed. There were many ways to put that puzzle together. Don't always settle for the first solution; explore the possibilities and then choose the best one.

SOMETIMES TEACHERS REPEAT THINGS!

SOMETIMES TEACHERS REPEAT THINGS!

Mr. R had a saying in his class: "If I repeat it three times, it will be on the test." Life often hands us a repeat. Some are pleasant—like the renewal of friendships. Others are not so pleasant. So, if you are living a redo, review what you have learned, think about what you can learn now, and enjoy all the memories. Sometimes even the unhappy memories end up having something good in them.

Above all, please believe in yourself. Don't let anyone or anything keep you from being all that you are. It's been said that "Your value doesn't decrease based on someone's inability to see your worth." You were created with a purpose and the talents to succeed in that purpose.

Sometimes you get a job and stay with it all your life. In our case, that never happened. Although leaving each job was difficult and sad, we knew God was leading us. That's why you need to pay attention to the road signs. Sometimes they say go, sometimes they can say wait, and sometimes there is a detour. Every move is designed to develop your talents and abilities. Sometimes the moves are so you can help others develop their talents.

Don't waste your life. Don't bemoan not being as smart, talented, or rich as _____ (fill in the blank). Be the best you that you can be today, and do better tomorrow.

HOMEWORK

You had to know the last thing would be this! So, here you are.

MATHEMATICS: Add a positive attitude; subtract negativity; count your blessings; divide time wisely.

HISTORY: Don't be afraid of the past, but learn from it during the present. It will make for a better future.

ENGLISH: Let your life have plenty of exclamation points and not too many fragments or run-ons.

READING: Spend time at the library exploring all the subjects not covered in the textbooks. Textbooks never tell all the stories. There are a lot of exciting stories and intriguing facts. Have an inquiring mind. Question the logic, and write down the quotes worth keeping. Maybe even memorize some!

SCIENCE: Breathe in the world around you. Feel the power of the wind, examine the cloudy sky, experience the effects of a fierce wind and a quiet breeze, and embrace the awe of the inky starlit universe. Listen to the sounds and the silence. Let them remind you Who is in charge and refresh your soul.

BIBLE: Study it well. Don't let others tell you what it says.

PE: Live life abundantly. Exercise your abilities. Smile!

Extra Credit: *Please know that whatever you have done or are doing, Mr. and Mrs. R will always love you. We are in the stands cheering you on. Keep in touch and let us know how you are doing. Blessings on you all.*

Mr. and Mrs. R

BULLETIN BOARD QUOTES

"Life is a song—sing it. Life is a game—play it. Life is a challenge—meet it. Life is a dream—realize it. Life is a sacrifice—offer it. Life is love—enjoy it."
—Sai Baba, Indian saint

"If you live long enough, you'll make mistakes. But if you learn from them, you'll be a better person. It's how you handle adversity, not how it affects you. The main thing is never quit, never quit, never quit."
—William J. Clinton, former US president

"When I hear somebody sigh, 'Life is hard,' I am always tempted to ask, 'Compared to what?'"
—Sydney J. Harris, American journalist

"'Finding yourself' is actually returning to yourself. An unlearning, an excavation, a remembering who you were before the world got its hands on you."
—Emily McDowell, founder of Em & Friends

"Don't take a bad path toward a good goal."
—Mrs. Robinson, educator

BULLETIN BOARD QUOTES

"Life's challenges are not supposed to paralyze you, they're supposed to help you discover who you are."
—Bernice Johnson Reagon, composer and activist

"Often people ask how I manage to be happy despite having no arms and no legs. The quick answer is that I have a choice. I can be angry about not having limbs, or I can be thankful that I have a purpose. I chose gratitude."
—Nick Vujicic, evangelist and motivational speaker

"Be true to yourself, help others, make each day your masterpiece, make friendship a fine art, drink deeply from good books—especially the Bible, build a shelter against a rainy day, give thanks for your blessings and pray for guidance every day."
—John Wooden, basketball coach

"Maybe it won't work out, maybe it won't be what you wanted, or it may just be the adventure of a lifetime. Take some chances."
—J. Mike Fields, life coach, speaker, and writer

ABOUT THE AUTHORS

ANDREW ROBINSON

Mr. Robinson grew up in Illinois near Chicago. He came to California to go to college, where he met Elda.

The couple were married in the summer of 1971 and graduated from Western (now Corban University in Salem, Oregon) in 1972. Following graduation, they moved to Wisconsin and worked at a home for mentally challenged children and adults.

They moved back to California in the summer of 1980 and began working in Christian schools in Northern California. Mr. Robinson received his ordination certificate in 1987 and received his master's in educational administration from Pensacola Christian School in 1989.

Mr. Robinson spent many summers umpiring softball as well as college baseball and softball. He continues to be an avid sports fan and memorabilia collector as well as a photographer. He did the photography for the book *A Simple Cup of Ty*.

Andrew Robinson can be reached at *mr.r.cares247365@gmail.com.*

ELDA ROBINSON

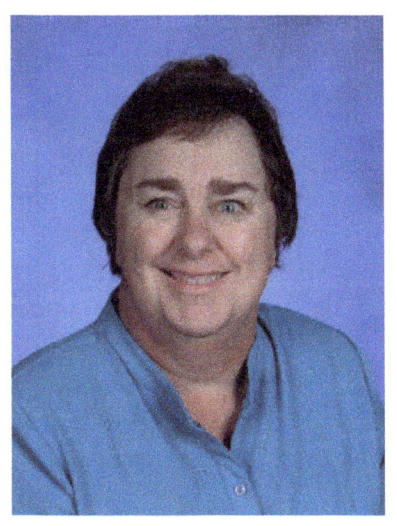

Mrs. Robinson grew up in a small town in Northern California. She went to Western Baptist Bible College in the fall of 1968. After marrying Andrew in 1971, she continued her schooling and graduated with Mr. Robinson in 1972. She worked at the home in Wisconsin for several years as well as teaching piano, volunteering at a retirement home, and being active in their church.

She began her teaching career when she moved back to California. Since receiving her master's in education from Phoenix University in 2003, she has co-authored science curricula, become a #1 international bestselling author, written the children's book *Nathanial's Family*, co-authored *Empowering You, Transforming Lives*, and authored *A Simple Cup of Ty*, for which Mr. Robinson did the photography.

Elda Robinson can be reached at ***mr.r.cares247365@gmail.com.***

REVIEWS

"When a teacher loves their students as if they are their own children, they see them more deeply, speak to them more wisely, and cherish them without end. This kind of love is conveyed in One More Thing."
—Shelby Kottemann, internationally bestselling author, Reiki master, and founder of Love's Nature LLC

"As someone who identifies as a lifelong learner, I fell in love with this book. The lessons and the messages are life-affirming and apply to everyone!"
—Misti Mazurik, lifelong learner and director of operations at RHG Media

"One More Thing is like a tiny little treasure chest of hidden gems that will shine and delight you—full of love and advice that comes in waves when you didn't realize you needed it. It brings hope to your heart and joy to your soul. Written from the wisdom and love of teachers who no doubt have inspired many of their students in times of need, this is a book I could read again and again and learn new things about myself each time."
—Tiffani Freckleton, RN; award-winning bestselling author of *My NICU Story: Written With Love*; contributor, *Letters to a Future Nurse*

"Dive into One More Thing for a treasure trove of wisdom on embracing positivity, learning from the past, and living with gratitude. This book is a must-read for inspiration in teaching and learning."
—Maureen Ryan Blake, founder, Maureen Ryan Blake Media

www.ingramcontent.com/pod-product-compliance
Lightning Source LLC
Chambersburg PA
CBHW070036040426
42333CB00040B/1694